All Things New

A Basic Training on the End Times

Rusty Hayes

www.sugarloafcc.org

All Things New
by Rusty Hayes

Printed in the United States of America

ISBN 1-60034-370-8

Cover image & design by Michael Largent, MLargent Design

www.xulonpress.com

Endorsements

Rusty Hayes has combined his biblical knowledge with his skills as a communicator to provide us with a practical study guide that will give any individual reader or study group a clearer understanding of the end times. Most importantly, Rusty's book emphasizes the hope and victory that belongs to every believer.

Steve Stroope, Senior Pastor of
Lake Pointe Church, Rockwall, Texas

Revelation...Prophecy...the words alone frighten many Christians into believing such things are just too mysterious, too complicated, and only for the realms of super theologians and spiritual giants. But Rusty Hayes has a different thought, "*...the Bible was meant to be understood...*" What a novel idea! *All Things New* presents the End Times in a way we all can understand, not as the final destination in our road to understanding, but more importantly, as the beginning.

Charles B. Graham,
Founder and Executive Director of CILOA;
Author of Take the Stand and A Year of Encouragement

I wholeheartedly endorse the book *All Things New* by the Right Reverend Bishop Russell Brian Hayes (a.k.a. "The Ragin' Cajun"). While I have not actually read the book, I am certain it carries sound theological doctrine such as, "aliens will take you to the mother ship at the next shooting star" and "salvation through chocolate". And let's not forget "grace through perfect Baptist preacher hair". These are sure to be the highlights of Reverend Bishop Hayes' masterful tome.

Sam O'Neal, married mother of two,
Administrative Assistant at Sugarloaf Community
Church; nickname— "Pitbull"

Dedication

This book is dedicated to the greatest wife on the planet, Judi Hayes, my priceless children: Olivia, Natalie, Juliette, and Joshua, the precious staff and people of Sugarloaf Community Church; and Dr. Bob Gullberg, who insisted I write a book some day during our many prayer times, dinners, coffee talks, and even physical exams! Bob, thanks for encouraging me to author even when I didn't know I could.

Acknowledgments

Special thanks to my research assistant, Deborah Schantz, for all the tireless effort she gives. You are a help sent from the Lord! Thanks also to my personal assistant, Sheila Long, without whom I would never have been organized enough to accomplish this work. Chuck Graham, lawyer, writer, and friend extraordinaire, also deserves many thanks for his very helpful insights. May your dreams of ministry come true and all your cases be won, especially if you're representing me! Who knows, maybe I plagiarized someone by accident! Keep your pencils sharpened, unless, or course, the rapture happens today.

Contents

Introduction

This book presents a very basic overview of the End Times for small groups, discipleship communities, or personal Bible study. My hope is to provide a helpful "big picture" approach to those of us who have been intimidated, overwhelmed, or flat-out scared to death of God's prophetic future. *All Things New* is not designed to offer an in-depth treatise on every theory found among the wide spectrum of eschatological (End Times) views. Nor is it an attempt to summarize and systematize all passages in the Bible related to prophecy. This work represents the efforts of a down-to-earth pastor attempting to capture, in a very user-friendly style, the basics of the End. It is presented from a dispensational, pretribulational, premillennial perspective. (For those of you who don't know what that means, don't worry, it's mentioned for the theological types among us who just can't live without big, hairy, technical words. I have now appeased my seminary brethren!) This book is also not an attempt to discredit or dishonor brothers and sisters in Christ who hold other views that fall under the umbrella of biblical faith. There are many great men and women of God who have different perspectives from my own. I should also say that I may be mistaken in my view. This book is certainly not the last word on this subject. By stating this, however, I am not suggesting that my view has no substance. Rest assured, the opinions of this book have been thoroughly researched and thoughtfully considered. My hope, however, is not to cause division, but to spur growth toward our precious Christ and offer a firmer grasp of His glorious plan for the ages. It's all about Jesus! If this book gives us all a greater appreciation of Him, regardless of our views of prophecy, it will have accomplished its purpose. To God be the glory!

CHAPTER 1

God's Big, Not-So-Scary Monster

Prophecy has always had a tremendous hold on my imagination. I can remember as a child thinking of the End Times as a mysterious, other-worldly, surreal mixture of bizarre images and strange creatures. It felt like a cross between *The Twilight Zone, The Wizard of Oz,* and scenes from *The Ten Commandments.* I was at times intensely fascinated, and at other times, uncomfortably frightened . . . and almost always confused.

In those early years, I was given the impression that the prophetic insights in Scripture were veiled in so much symbolism that end time mysteries were too hidden to understand or too vague to comprehend. Only the overall theme of the triumph of good over evil was clear. Despite the fact that roughly a fourth of the Bible is prophetic, I was left with the impression that this huge percentage of revelation was a sort of secret code that was very important, but inaccessible.

Emotionally, biblical prophecy was like the Loch Ness Monster—a giant something-or-other swimming under the currents of faith, yet seldom explained, vaguely understood, and certainly not captured. I was fascinated by it, but very leery of swimming in its dark waters. My primary emotion:

FEAR! It flat-out scared me like demon possession and my uncle's false teeth. Prophecy was a Stephen King movie with a horrifying ending. I tended to avoid it.

My guess is that many of you feel the same way. Books like Ezekiel, Daniel, Zechariah, and especially Revelation are filed somewhere in your mind under the heading: Sacred, Supernatural, Secret, and Scary! Prophecy has been the dark stained-glass window of the Bible to you, offering only glimpses of light. You can make out certain images, but most of it seems eerily hidden in the shadows.

I can relate. But something wonderful has happened to me since those early days. About 13 years ago, I decided to dive into the Loch and give the Monster another look. Except this time I studied it in the same way I studied any other subject in the Bible. Instead of looking for hidden, spiritualized meanings and secret messages, I examined it at face value. As with any other sacred text, I let the Word of God speak for itself. If the Scriptures interpreted an image as symbolic, I took the image as such. If the text explained the image elsewhere, I accepted the explanation. I also studied under some great scholars like Drs. John Walvoord, Dwight Pentecost, Robert Lightner, Warren Wiersbe, and Roy Zuck. These theologians and Bible teachers approached the Bible in a common-sense way. They studied the Scriptures with the idea that the Bible is meant to be understood and is written with plain truth in mind. God's Word isn't some kind of ancient code written only for elites or mystics. The Lord gave us His Word to reveal His ways to us. Prophecy is no exception.

Over time, I've come to some exciting conclusions. In this study, I'd like to share with you some of these encouraging insights. As we embark on our journey, let me give you a few guiding principles that will help us find our way to a better understanding of God's future.

Four Truths About the End Times

1. In order to understand biblical prophecy, we need to understand how the End Times fit into God's overall plan for history.

God has always had a plan for history. History is literally "His Story." He invented time and is in control of all that happens within it (and without it for that matter!). Often, in the circumstances of life, we forget how BIG God is. He's **HUGE**! There is no rain drop, no flake of snow, no rotation around the sun, and no change in temperature that is out of God's control. The next breath you breathe will happen by His will. He owns existence! So the End Times are no surprise to Him. I don't know about you, but that comforts me. Think about it. The same God who invited children to sit on His lap. The same God who touched the sick and suffering. The same God who was known as "a friend of sinners." The same God who loves us more than we love our own children. The same God who died on a cross for our sins. This same loving, forgiving, redeeming God, our Lord Jesus Christ, is in control! The Bible says in Colossians 1:16 that everything and everyone was created by Him and for Him. Take a look:

> *For by him all things were created: things in heaven and on earth, visible and invisible, whether thrones or powers or rulers or authorities; all things were created by him and for him. Col. 1:16 (NIV)*

Wow! He really is **HUGE**! In the Book of Revelation, it's clear that time itself is in His control. Check it out:

> *"I am the Alpha and the Omega," says the Lord God, "who is, and who was, and who is to come, the Almighty." Revelation 1:8 (NIV)*

17

Jesus states here that He is the Alpha and the Omega. These are the first and last letters of the Greek alphabet. He's basically saying, "I am the beginning of everything and control its ending; I own history." I like how Peterson's translation says this:

> *The Master declares, "I'm A to Z. I'm THE GOD WHO IS, THE GOD WHO WAS, AND THE GOD ABOUT TO ARRIVE. I'm the Sovereign-Strong." Rev. 1:8 (The Message)*

Jesus is the Sovereign-Strong. He's Sovereign—in control of everything, and He's Strong—truly God Almighty. Allow that to sink in for a moment. Jesus, the One we celebrate every year at Christmas and at Easter. The same kind God our children say grace to before meals. The same bleeding sacrifice that Mel Gibson displayed in *The Passion*. This same gentle, forgiving, precious God is the Programmer behind this giant software package we call history.

There's a lot of comfort in that realization. Let me give you an example. Recently, I was watching the news and heard about a little girl who was abducted and murdered viciously. The details grieved me deeply. Such hideous evil is incredibly difficult for me to grasp. How can wickedness be allowed to function at such wretched depths? I thought of my own daughters and how precious they are to me and my heart was wrenched. I couldn't bear to continue watching the story. But then the thought hit me: *God is still in control. Christ will right this wrong.* As a matter of fact, if Jesus is truly in control, He'll right all wrongs. Somehow, in some miraculous way that we can't understand, He'll reverse every evil act and make Satan regret ever unleashing such cruelty on the planet. I don't know how He'll do it, but I know He will. I don't understand why evil is allowed to spike at various times in history, but I know that God will completely demolish it one day. And the reason I know this is because, as we'll see repeatedly, He is HUGE and bigger than anything evil can throw at us. I have no doubt I'll see that little girl in Heaven one day and she won't be troubled one bit by her pain on this planet. God will magnificently restore her and we'll all be gloriously blessed. There is a plan, and it's a good one! What hope we have in Jesus!

2. The message of world history, from the beginning to the end, is: **GOD IS THE GREATEST!!!**

History isn't just a series of chance happenings with no rhyme or reason. There is a point! God has, is, and will say something through history. And that overarching message is "God is the greatest!" Look at Ephesians 1:11-12 in the Living Bible:

> *". . . all things happen just as he decided long ago.*
> *12 God's purpose in this was that we should praise*
> *God and give glory to him . . ." Ephesians 1:11-12*
> *(TLB)*

God has a plan, the plan has a purpose, and the purpose is praise! He has orchestrated all of history—the beginning, middle, and end—to say one thing in loud, bold letters: **GOD IS THE GREATEST!!!** When it's all said and done, we will praise God and give Him the glory due His name. As a matter of fact, even the forces of evil will fall in awe before Him. Soak in the promise we have in Romans 14:11

> *" 'As I live and breathe,' God says,*
> *'every knee will bow before me;*
> *every tongue will tell the honest truth*
> *that I and only I am God.' " (The Message)*

There is only one God, and despite all the bad that happens in this world, good will not only prevail, it will totally domi- nate! God will correct all wrongs and retroactively right every single violation of goodness. And all creation, both material and spiritual, will recognize that He alone is the King.

I love what David says in Psalm 77 when he looks at God's hand in history:

> *Once again I'll go over what GOD has done,*
> *lay out on the table the ancient wonders;*
> *12I'll ponder all the things you've accomplished,*
> *and give a long, loving look at your acts.*
> *13Oh God! Your way is holy!*
> *No god is great like God! Psalm 77:11-13*
> *(The Message)*

One of the reasons Bible study is so nourishing to the soul is that it presents history from Heaven's view. We see what God sees in the sacred pages. We understand that His hand was moving before we were just a twinkle in our parents' eyes. He knows what's going on in our world and is in complete control. No other being can claim such absolute power. Nothing compares to the grandeur of GOD. And as we take "a long loving look" at His acts in the future, our goal is not to stroke our egos with more knowledge or to find a new hobby in "prophecy speculation." No, our goal is to grow closer to our Lord and gain greater awe for our magnificent King.

3. There is a difference between the nation of Israel and the Church. Both, however, make up the people of God and, therefore, have overlapping promises.

Have you ever wondered why we have an Old Testament and a New Testament? Why don't we just have the Bible without this division? Is it for an intermission? When you're finished reading the Old Testament, are you supposed to go to the concession stand for Gummi Bears™ and stretch your legs before getting into the New Testament? Or does it say something?

Well, actually, there's a good reason for the division. It suggests that something has changed in God's program for history. The word "testament" is another word for "covenant" or "arrangement." In the Old Testament, God established an actual holy nation from which to display His greatness and reveal Himself to the world. That nation was Israel. He made a covenant with the Hebrews to be their God in a unique, glorifying way. An early statement of this covenant is found in Genesis 12:1-3:

> The LORD had said to Abram, "Leave your country,
> your people and your father's household and go to
> the land I will show you.
> ²"I will make you into a great nation
>   and I will bless you;
> I will make your name great,
>   and you will be a blessing.
> ³I will bless those who bless you,
>   and whoever curses you I will curse;
> and all peoples on earth
>   will be blessed through you." Genesis 12:1-3 (NIV)

Theologians refer to this promise as the Abrahamic Covenant and it was the first of several major covenants God made with Israel in mind. Notice that God promises that something new is going to be made, a great nation that will bless the world. We'll examine this in more detail later, but suffice it to say that Abraham's lineage would be no ordinary nation. God had plans for Israel, and these plans consisted of nothing less than touching the entire world.

The New Testament opened up a new relationship between God and humanity. With the coming of Christ, God extended an intimate relationship to not only the Hebrews, but also to any person of any country and race in the world. A new age of grace had dawned that was unheard of in the Old Testament. For the first time in history, all people could approach God with equal access!

This is talked about in Ephesians 3. The Apostle Paul speaks of a "mystery" that was unknown to the Israelites (and indeed to the world) in the Old Testament. Today, that mystery is revealed. Look at Paul's words:

> *I was chosen to explain to everyone this plan that God, the Creator of all things, had kept secret from the beginning.*
>
> *[10]God's purpose was to show his wisdom in all its rich variety to all the rulers and authorities in the heavenly realms. They will see this when Jews and Gentiles are joined together in his church. [11]This was his plan from all eternity, and it has now been carried out through Christ Jesus our Lord.*
>
> *[12]Because of Christ and our faith in him, we can now come fearlessly into God's presence, assured of his glad welcome. Ephesians 3:9-12 (NLT)*

It's clear from the passage that God had a secret plan at work in the Old Testament. The plan was to create a new family that welcomed people of all races into fellowship with Him. That family is the Church. Christ's death on the cross and resurrection from the dead opened up new horizons that were previously unimaginable. We, people who are not of Israel (i.e. Gentiles), *can now come fearlessly into God's presence, assured of his glad welcome!* What a wonderful blessing! The New Testament emphasizes this new arrangement.

Let's pause for a moment here and examine this a bit. Why is there a new arrangement? How did God work all this out? Well, if you read through the Old Testament, you will notice major sections of it that are legal in nature. For example, the books of Exodus, Leviticus, Numbers and Deuteronomy give all kinds of regulations concerning society and proper forms of worship. You'll also notice in these chapters that there are frequent references to blood and sacrifice. Leviticus 3 is a good example:

> *If he offers a lamb, he is to present it before the LORD.*
> *⁸He is to lay his hand on the head of his offering*
> *and slaughter it in front of the Tent of Meeting. Then*
> *Aaron's sons shall sprinkle its blood against the altar*
> *on all sides. Leviticus 3:7-8 (NIV)*

Why the emphasis on sacrifice and blood? Well, the Bible teaches that sin is, among others things, a debt (see Matthew 6:12: "forgive us our debts"). When we violate goodness in any way, we owe the Author of goodness a payment. Something has to give to make restitution for this violation. And God says that blood must be shed as that payment. Take a look at Hebrews 9:22.

> *In fact, we can say that according to the law of*
> *Moses, nearly everything was purified by sprinkling*
> *with blood. Without the shedding of blood, there is no*
> *forgiveness of sins. Hebrews 9:22 (NLT)*

In the Old Testament, God established a nation to display this principle. That nation was Israel. He also created a complex system of rules to illustrate the tragedy of sin. That system was known as "the Law" and it provided detailed instructions as to the severity of individual sins and the sacrifices required to satisfy their debts. The problem was, however, that no one could keep up with its demands. The fact of the matter was, and is, that there's too much sin for us to keep up with. No sacrifice was available to atone for all the debt! The Law taught us that the world desperately needed a Savior, someone who could handle the tremendous, infinite debt of our sins. But where was such a powerful, pure sacrifice to be found? Where could we find such a "lamb?" Well, we didn't have to find Him. The Father did. And the Lamb's name is Jesus Christ!

Check out what Galatians 3 says:

Therefore the Law has become our tutor to lead us to Christ, that we may be justified by faith. [25]But now that faith has come, we are no longer under a tutor. Galatians 3:24-25 (NASB)

Here's the thing. God never intended the Law to rescue the Israelites, or anyone else for that matter, from sin. Instead, He designed it as a massive illustration of how futile it is for flawed humanity to try and earn forgiveness from the Almighty. We're just too peppered with sin to make it work. So, in essence, the Old Testament and its Law teach us that we all desperately need a Savior. It's like the Law is Aretha Franklin and it's singing throughout the Old Testament "Rescue Me!!!!" The Law is a "tutor" that leads us to get over ourselves and run to Christ for help. And Jesus is the fulfillment of this function.

The death and resurrection of Christ fulfilled the Law on a number of levels. Of primary importance is the fact that Jesus' death fulfilled all its requirements. Because He was both God and man, His sacrifice paid for humanity's sins perfectly. He could legitimately represent humanity because He was fully human. His sacrifice was also infinitely perfect and satisfactory because He was God. His death alone paid the debt. How precious is the blood of Christ!

Now there is a new arrangement in place. We access God not by a Law or by human effort; we access Him by faith. Our sins are paid for and the Law is appeased. But, we don't have the benefit of this wonderful state unless we have faith in Christ. And faith simply means we believe He was who He said He was, we trust in what He said He did, and we live how He said to live. Faith means "to trust fully."

Notice what Ephesians 2:8-9 says:

For it is by grace you have been saved, through faith—and this not from yourselves, it is the gift of God—9not by works, so that no one can boast. Ephesians 2:8-9 (NIV)

The word "grace" means "love that we don't deserve; unmerited favor." Our rescue from sin, our salvation, is not something we deserve. It isn't accomplished by following some code of conduct or by being a good person. It is paid for by the blood of Christ and is accepted through faith. Now, I don't know about you, but that is such a relief to me! I'm such a rascal at times that there is no question in my mind that I wouldn't make it to Heaven if it depended on me. And I'm a pastor! I'm paid to be good. It's my living! If you're not a pastor, you have to be good for free. As one pastor said, "You guys are good for nothing!" Isn't it wonderful to have a Savior who operates on grace? Amazing grace, how sweet the sound!

Now, back to the distinction between Israel and the Church. The Old Testament has Israel as a dominant theme and the New Testament has the Church as a dominant theme. Israel is created by God in Genesis 12, the Church is created by God in Acts 2. Both share Jesus as the Savior. Both get to Heaven because of His death on the cross. Both can be called the People of God. However, there are some plans God has for each that are unique. National Israel still has a prophetic future, as does the Church. Often the question is asked, "What if an Israelite becomes a Christian; is she seen by God as an Israelite or a member of the Church?" Well, at this point in history, she is seen primarily as a member of the Church. Anyone, whether Jew or Gentile, who accepts Christ as her Savior is brought into His Body, the Church, and she will be part of God's plan for the Church. National Israel, however, still has a distinct future with distinct promises (which we will cover later in the book). For our purposes, keep in mind that it's very important to recognize that there are two prophetic programs at work in history right now: one for Israel and one for the Church. And, in the end, both of them will say, **"GOD IS THE GREATEST!!!"**

4. God has divided history into various "ages" that are characterized by unique ways of relating to Him.

Great scholars have debated the number of ages (also known as "dispensations") and how they are specifically divided, but there is no question that history can be broken down into distinct, God-designed segments with their own set of characteristics.

The Apostle Paul refers to future "ages" in Ephesians 2:7; and in Colossians 1:26 he speaks of past "ages." These periods were characterized by distinct ways of relating to God that differed, sometimes drastically, from one another.

For our purposes, I've broken down history into two infinite periods and seven ages in order for us to gain a grasp of biblical prophecy. The ages are listed in chart form on the following page. They consist of Eternity Past, the Age of Innocence, the Age of Conscience, the Age of Government, the Age of Promise, the Age of Law, the Age of Grace, the Age of the Future Kingdom, and Eternity Future. Each of these periods has at least one corresponding covenant associated with it. We'll look at each one of these briefly and then spend the majority of our study on the Age of the Future Kingdom.

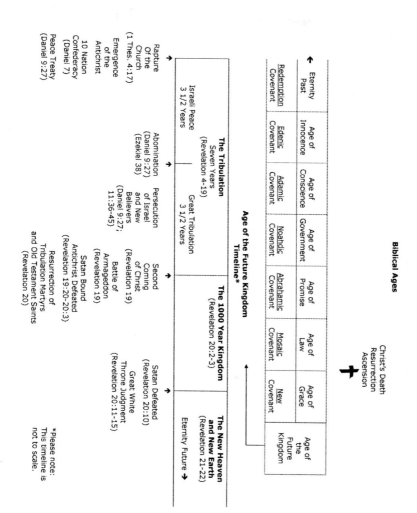

Eternity Past

This period refers to time before the creation of the world. We have no indication of its length, and may not even be able to grasp it. Existence and time itself were created during this period. We know that the angels were created during this time and that Satan's rebellion probably occurred then. We also know that God was planning our future redemption at this time. Titus 1:1-2 refers to eternity past as "before the beginning of time" and indicates that God established "the hope of eternal life" then. The writer of Hebrews speaks of the "eternal covenant" that was fulfilled in the blood of Christ (Hebrews 13:20). The word translated "eternal" can have the connotation of "perpetual" with an idea of the past in mind. In other words, God established His plan of rescuing the human race through Jesus before anything was even created! This plan is known as the Redemption Covenant and it was made within the Trinity. God the Father, God the Son, and God the Holy Spirit knew that we as human beings would mess up our lives, our souls, and our world. So the Trinity came up with a plan in which the Son would die for our sins. Isn't God awesome!

The Age of Innocence (Genesis 1-3)

This period is characterized by purity. God creates the world without sin. Adam and Eve are crafted in His image and walk closely with Him in a perfect garden home. Life is wonderful. There is no violence, disease, or animosity. Humanity is spectacular! Adam and Eve have a perfect marriage, perfect health, superhuman abilities, and display all the characteristics of the human race at its best. They have but one rule to follow: Don't eat of the tree. In Genesis 2:16-17, God states clearly, *"You are free to eat from any tree in the garden; [17]but you must not eat from the tree of the knowledge of good and evil, for when you eat of it you will surely die."* This was an agreement, a covenant if you will, that, as we all know, was broken after Satan tempted Adam and Eve to fall. The covenant is known as the Edenic Covenant. After it was broken, the world became a far more dangerous place. And, as Pastor Andy Stanley (an excellent Bible preacher) has pointed out, due to its hazardous nature, it became a world in need of more rules.

The Age of Conscience (Genesis 3-8)

The next period is characterized by the need to discern good from evil more skillfully. Humanity has to utilize conscience more than when the world was without sin. We see the first instance of death during this period as animals are killed to cover Adam and Eve. For the first time in their lives, they need protection against the elements and experience shame. God also recognizes that Adam and Eve now know what evil is and must be discerning to navigate around the pitfalls of further sin. An arrangement, the Adamic Covenant, is established and referred to in Genesis 3:21-22: *The Lord God made garments of skin for Adam and his wife and clothed them. [22]And the Lord said, "the man has now become like one of us, knowing good and evil."* The implication of this passage is that humanity is now operating under conscience, or with a capacity to distinguish between good and evil.

The Age of Government (Genesis 8-11)

As the population of the planet increases, sin increases as well. Sin's destructive effects on society must be curtailed. Government, therefore, is established by the hand of God (see Romans 13:1-5). During this period, God singles out Noah and reestablishes order on the planet. In an act of grace, He makes a covenant with Noah that blesses the rest of history: *[7]As for you, be fruitful and increase in number; multiply the earth and increase upon it. [9]I establish my covenant with you: [11]Never again will all life be cut off by the waters of a flood; never again will there be a flood to destroy the earth. Genesis*

9:7, 11 (NIV). This is known as the Noahdic Covenant and is still in effect today. The earth will be destroyed in the future, but it won't be by a flood. Every time we see a rainbow, as Dr. Warren Wiersbe (a well-respected Bible teacher/scholar) says, we see God's signature on this Covenant.

The Age of Promise (Genesis 11-Exodus 19)

After the flood, the human race begins to spread again. The era of the patriarchs (early fathers of Israel and other countries) begins and God separates people groups into individual nations. Out of the East, God calls Abraham (also called Abram) to begin His new chosen people, the nation of Israel. Several times, God promises Abraham a great posterity. He will have many descendants who will inherit vast tracts of land. Indeed, all the Middle East will one day be theirs and God will establish them as an eternal kingdom. One instance of this promise is in Genesis 15:18*: On that day the Lord made a covenant with Abram and said, "To your descendants I give this land, from the river of Egypt to the great river, the Euphrates."* This promise is one part of the Abrahamic Covenant mentioned earlier that is still in effect today. That is to say, one day God will establish national Israel all the way from Egypt to Iraq. And it will be a nation whose borders will never be taken.

The Age of Law (Exodus 19-Malachi)

Once the nation of Israel is established, God issues a detailed series of laws regulating life for His people, the core of which are the timeless moral principles of the Ten Commandments (which I believe are still in effect today as healthy rules for life). Israel is to follow every law perfectly in order to stay in God's favor. Large portions of the Old Testament show the highs and lows of the nation floundering between seasons of obedience, blessing, rebellion, judgment, and repentance. Prophets are raised up to point the people back to conformity with the Law. Yet over and over again, the nation fails to live righteously. Exodus 34:27-28 is one place where the primary covenant of the period, the Mosaic Covenant, is described: *Then the Lord said to Moses, "Write down these words, for in accordance with these words I have made a covenant with you and with Israel." . . .²⁸ and he wrote on the tablets the words of the covenant—the Ten Commandments.* When Jesus arrived on the scene, the Law was still in effect. Jesus Himself observed the Law perfectly. He was the only person who ever lived who fulfilled it, every single comma and period. Wow! What an awesome Lord we serve!

The Age of Grace (Matthew 1-Revelation 5)

We are living in this age even as I write! It began the moment Jesus entered our world through the virgin Mary and continues to bless us in our time. This age is characterized by the unmerited favor and love of the Father toward a world that desperately needs Him. The benefits of salvation and intimate communion with God are available to all due to the blood of Christ and His remarkable sacrifice on our behalf. At any moment, anywhere, people can come to know God at the deepest level. The Gospel ("good news") that God forgives and cleanses sin is openly declared. The Church has been established by Christ, animated by God's own Holy Spirit, and comprised of sinners from every nationality and walk of life who have been forgiven through faith because of the grace of God. What a blessing it is to be born during such a time as this! The primary covenant of this period is known as the New Covenant. With respect to Israel, it is articulated in Jeremiah 31:31-33: *³¹"The time is coming," declares the Lord, "when I will make a new covenant with the house of Israel and with the house of Judah. ³²It will not be like the covenant I made with their forefathers when I took them by*

31

the hand to lead them out of Egypt, because they broke my covenant, though I was a husband to them," declares the Lord. [33] *"This is the covenant I will make with the house of Israel after that time," declares the Lord. "I will put my law in their minds and write it on their hearts. I will be their God and they will be my people."* (emphasis mine). The offer for this covenant to be fulfilled happened when Jesus made Himself known as the Messiah to Israel. Israel, however, rejected Him as their King (see Matthew 23:37-39). Therefore, the benefits of this covenant went to the Church. Take a look at Luke 22:19-20 which shows that the Lord's Supper commemorates God's new covenant with the Church: *And he took bread, gave thanks and broke it, and gave it to them, saying, "This is my body given for you; do this in remembrance of me."* [20]*In the same way, after the supper he took the cup, saying, "This cup is the <u>new covenant</u> in my blood, which is poured out for you"* (emphasis mine).

Soon, the new "body" of the Church would be created and the body and blood of Christ would enable members of it to actually have the Holy Spirit dwell in their hearts and inform their consciences. Truly, God's moral principles would be written "on their hearts." The nation of Israel has yet to accept this covenant, but it will in the future. This covenant is one place where the Church and Israel overlap.

The Age of the Future Kingdom

The age that is yet to happen is the Age of the Future Kingdom. It consists of three distinct sections: The Tribulation, The Millennial Kingdom (or The 1000-Year Kingdom), and The New Heaven and New Earth. We will spend the majority of our study in this period. Both the Abrahamic Covenant and the New Covenant will find final fulfillment for Israel during this time.

Eternity Future (same as The New Heaven and New Earth)

Eternity Future is another name for the final section of the Age of the Future Kingdom. I mention it here only to highlight that it will be infinite and similar in scope to Eternity Past. In a very real sense, all of history since Genesis 1 to the present is a small dot on the timeline of eternity. We will live far longer after death than before. Therefore, it is fitting that we study what the future holds. God wrote His Word for us to understand, so let's dive in! The rest of our study will examine the major events of the Future Kingdom Age in the order of their occurrence. Fasten your seatbelts!

Study Questions:

1. Share with your group one of the first times you thought about the end times. What were your emotions? What did you understand, and what were you clueless about?

2. Read Psalm 96, which contains prophetic elements.
    *   What is the tone of this psalm and how does it affect your view of the end?
    *   What are some of the actions we're supposed to do as His people according to this psalm?
    *   Why, do you think, is nature (trees, the sea, etc.) mentioned here? (see Romans 8:18-21 for more discussion)

3. As you consider the Ages of History, what strikes you about yourself and about God? Do the Ages have anything in common? What would you say are the two or three most prominent Ages of History?

CHAPTER 2

Are you Ready? (The Rapture)

One of the main fears people have about the end of the world is "Will I survive it?" Often the question is posed as, "Am I good enough for God's protection? Will God choose to help me; or should I expect to be destroyed in a plague, a violent execution, or a war? Will locusts infest me and meteors pummel my head? How can I know that I'm okay with God? Will I make it?" These are all legitimate fears. The end is coming, and much of it won't be pretty. As we will see, the Bible teaches that massive chunks of the planet with be scorched and millions upon millions will die horrific deaths. If you don't know where you are in the equation, it can be bone-chilling to think about the future. So let's make sure we're on God's side when all Heaven literally breaks loose, shall we?

The Rapture and Why You Want A Reservation

The term "rapture" refers to the unpredictable, quick, and dramatic disappearance of the Church caused by the mid-air return of Jesus. Its purpose is nothing short of actually taking believers to Heaven and protecting us from God's future world-wide wrath! It's a divine rescue operation! Those who are not raptured will experience excruciating pain in the worst judgment this planet has ever known.

A primary passage on the rapture is 1 Thessalonians 4:13-18. The context has to do with members of the early church at Thessalonica who were grieving over their dead. Apparently, other members of the church had passed away and those who remained alive worried about their deceased loved ones with respect to the rapture. Would believers who died miss out on the rapture? And if so, what fate awaited them? The Apostle Paul comforts these worried believers with these words:

> *Brothers, we do not want you to be ignorant about those who fall asleep, or to grieve like the rest of men, who have no hope.* [14]*We believe that Jesus died and rose again and so we believe that God will bring with Jesus those who have fallen asleep in him.* [15]*According to the Lord's own word, we tell you that we who are still alive, who are left till the coming of the Lord, will certainly not precede those who have fallen asleep.* [16]*For the Lord himself will come down from heaven, with a loud command, with the voice of the archangel and with the trumpet call of God, and the dead in Christ will rise first.* [17]*After that, we who are still alive and are left will be <u>caught up</u>* (in the Latin translation, this is the word "raptos," which is where we get the term "rapture" in English) *together with them in the clouds to meet the Lord in the air. And so we will be with the Lord forever.* [18]*Therefore encourage each other with these words* (comments and emphasis mine). *1 Thessalonians 4:13-18 (NIV)*

Notice, St. Paul says we are not "to grieve like the rest of men, who have no hope." This information he gives concerning the end times is encouraging, not terrifying.

When we talk about the end as believers, we're not to be fearful or in a state of anxiety. Something good is coming for those who trust Jesus! Verse 14 is a key to understanding this concept. Those who believe in Christ have nothing to worry about. Paul clearly says, "We believe that Jesus died and rose again . . ." So, the litmus test of those who have this hope is belief in Jesus Christ and the Gospel. If you are a believer, you have hope to look forward to, not destruction.

Now, what is this hope? Well, quite simply, it's the rapture. If you know Christ, you have a reservation. Take a look at v. 17. After Paul tells the Thessalonians that the Lord is coming back, he clearly says all believers at that time (including dead believers) will be "caught up together with them in the clouds to meet the Lord in the air." Then we'll "be with the Lord forever." The phrase translated "caught up" is the term *raptos* in Latin and *harpazo* in Greek, and it has the idea of "being plucked up and taken away." God is going to take His Church away from the world at this time. And the event will actually cause us to fly! The text says we'll "meet the Lord in the air." Wow! I can't wait! Ever since I was a little boy, I've been a fan of Superman. I love the way he can fly. As a matter of fact, when I was a little guy, I fervently prayed that God would make me into Superman. This passage promises that one day God will answer my prayer! I'll fly like a super-hero and actually defy gravity! And no amount of kryptonite will hurt me! I will literally go up, up, and away!

The Timing of the Rapture

So when will it happen? How will we know when the rapture will take place? Well, Scripture indicates that it will happen without any immediate indication. In other words, there won't be a headline in the papers saying, "Rapture Scheduled on June 3 at 4:00 pm." The sky won't turn green and Oprah won't be announcing it on television. It will come quickly and without warning. Theologians refer to this as "imminence." The rapture will be imminent, unpredictable, and without precise foreknowledge.

1 Corinthians 15:51-52 describes it this way:

> *But let me tell you a wonderful secret God has revealed to us. Not all of us will die, but we will all be transformed. [52]It will happen in a moment, in the blinking of an eye, when the last trumpet is blown. For when the trumpet sounds, the Christians who have died will be raised with transformed bodies. And then we who are living will be transformed so that we will never die. 1 Cor. 15:51-52 (NLT)*

God's Word says this spectacular event will happen instantaneously, "in the blinking of an eye." How fast can you blink your eye? Not too long ago, I painfully attempted to wear hard contact lenses. My eye doctor recommended them to me because of the irregular shape of my eyes. As I was learning to put them in, I found out very quickly that the eye is actually quicker than the hand. My eyelids were so fast! I couldn't get those accursed lenses from Hades into my eyes! The rapture will be like my eyelids. In a millisecond, this event will hit. And the text says we'll be changed. When Jesus escorts us to Heaven, we'll have "transformed bodies" that will be immortal. We really will be like Superman! After this happens, I'm going to ask my brother, Steve, to shoot me just to see what it feels like to have bullets bounce off my chest!

Jesus also said that He has custom-built homes that He is preparing even now for us to occupy after the rapture. In John 14:2-3 He encourages us that He's coming back to get us and take us to a personalized, celestial mansion:

> *In my Father's house are many mansions: if it were not so, I would have told you. I go to prepare a place*

*for you. ³And if I go and prepare a place for you, I will
come again, and receive you unto myself; that where
I am, there ye may be also. John 14:2-3 (KJV)*

What a joy to know that Jesus has not only taken care of my
sins, He's also assured my prophetic future! As believers, we
have no need to fear the end of the world, for it's simply a new
beginning of joy for us! We're headed back to the Garden, but
this time there are castles in it with our names on them.

Have you ever noticed that we seem to be fascinated
with castles? Just a cursory glance at our great stories indicates that there is something about these mansions that
intrigues us. Even Superman has his castle, "The Fortress of
Solitude!" Whether it's the spired emblem of Walt Disney
World, the Elfin architecture of *The Lord of the Rings*, the
Jedi cathedrals of *Star Wars*, or the enchanted kingdoms of
The Chronicles of Narnia, we adore castles. Could it be that
somewhere inside of us we know that our proper abode is
celestial? Perhaps our instincts tell us that we weren't made
for a sinful world of crumbling institutions and decaying
shelters. Maybe, just maybe, we were designed for glory.
And one day, if you're a believer, you'll be home! That
brings tears to my eyes. Praise God!

So, back to the question, when will it be? Well, we don't
know the exact time of the rapture, but we do have an idea of
its place in the sequence of End-Time events. It's logical to
conclude that it will mark the beginning of the end. Let me
give you several reasons why I hold this view.

First, the descriptions of the rapture present it as an
event that is unpredictable. In the above quote of Jesus
from John 14:2-3, it's interesting to note that Jesus doesn't
make mention of any event happening before His rapture.
He simply says, "I will come back and take you to be with
me . . .". This seems rather curious if there was to be a time
of wrath (the Tribulation) on the planet before He comes.

Jesus doesn't say, "Hey, listen, you're going to go through a terrible time of judgment (the Great Tribulation), face Satan and the Antichrist as they take over the world, and experience the last and most devastating World War in history (the Battle of Armageddon), and then I'll come and get you." No, Jesus simply says that He is currently preparing a place for us and that He'll come back to bring us there. Add to this the 1 Corinthians 15:52 description of the rapture as sudden and without warning (see also 1 Thes. 5:1-3 below), and the timing seems clear. The rapture apparently takes place before the Tribulation, otherwise it would be predictable, foreseeable, and come with plenty of warning. Since the Tribulation is exactly seven years (more on this later), scholars could calculate the exact time of a post-Tribulation rapture. They would simply have to start the clock after the Tribulation begins. But, remember, the rapture is described in the passages already cited as imminent, unpredictable, and without precise foreknowledge. So, there is good reason to believe it will happen before the Tribulation.

Another reason to believe the rapture will begin the end times sequence is that it is clearly linked to rescuing the Church from End Times judgment. Paul discusses the coming wrath that will be the end of the world in 1 Thessalonians 1 and makes some very insightful comments about its timing:

> . . . *for they themselves report what kind of reception you gave us. They tell how you turned to God from idols to serve the living and true God, *[10]*and to wait for his Son from heaven, whom he raised from the dead—Jesus, who rescues us from the coming wrath.* 1 Thes. 1:9-10 (NIV)

Check out the timing of "the coming wrath" at the end of v. 10. It comes <u>after</u> Jesus "rescues us." Look at the passage again, . . . *Jesus, who rescues us from the coming wrath.* There is a "rescuing" that happens with the Church that prevents us from experiencing the coming horrific wrath of God. Now, look at how St. Paul describes this time of wrath in 1 Thessalonians 5:1-3. He begins with what unbelievers can expect:

When is all this going to happen? I really don't need to say anything about that, dear brothers, ²for you know perfectly well that no one knows. That day of the Lord will come unexpectedly, like a thief in the night. ³When people are saying, "All is well; everything is quiet and peaceful"—then, all of a sudden, disaster will fall upon them as suddenly as a woman's birth pains begin when her child is born. And these people will not be able to get away anywhere—there will be no place to hide. 1 Thessalonians 5:1-3 (TLB)

The people in this passage are unbelievers and they'll be hit hard, without warning. They will be complacent and feel like everything is hunky-dory when disaster will strike with shocking force. It will be similar to a pregnant woman's labor pains.

Judi and I have four children and I can still remember the sudden pains Judi experienced with each one of those pregnancies. There were times when she'd experience enormous jolts of agony. The pain surged out of nowhere. And her pain became my pain very quickly if I didn't have a helpful attitude! That's how it will be for those who mock God. Instant, shocking pain. And the passage says "there will be no place to hide" for them.

But what about us? Well, Paul goes on to contrast our future with these unbelievers. In v. 4, he states:

But you, brethren, are not in darkness, that the day should overtake you like a thief. 1 Thessalonians 5:4 (NASB)

Then he goes on to state quite clearly where we stand in vv. 9-11:

> *For God did not appoint us to suffer wrath but to receive salvation through our Lord Jesus Christ. [10]He died for us so that, whether we are awake or asleep, we may live together with him. [11]Therefore encourage one another and build each other up, just as in fact you are doing. 1 Thessalonians 5:9-11 (NIV)*

We aren't on the lookout for a day that will take us over like a thief and shock us in judgment. We are to hope in a miraculous rescue, the rapture! God did not "appoint us to suffer wrath." This word is to encourage us as we move ever closer to the end of days.

A final compelling reason to hold that the rapture inaugurates the end times is that there are no passages (absolutely none!) that refer to the Church in the end time judgment known as the Great Tribulation (we'll discuss the Great Trib. later in the study). For example, Revelation chapters 5-19 describe the whirlwind of judgment the world is yet to reap, yet it never mentions the word "Church" in any of its disturbing pronouncements. If the Church was an object of God's wrath in these chapters, then surely it would have been described clearly as such. This argument is all the more compelling since the term "church" is used frequently in Revelation 2-3, which happen before the Tribulation. The probability is that the Church has been raptured before the judgments of chapters 5-19.

Study Questions:

1. Look over the passages we examined in this chapter and discuss how they touch you. What insights do they give you about the nature of salvation and what it means to believe in Jesus? What do they say about grace (the way God loves us when we don't deserve it)?

2. What will you do with the information you've learned in this lesson? What does it matter to your daily life? Be specific.

3. Read all of 1 Thessalonians 5:1-11 and discuss at least five descriptions that should characterize our lives as believers and how to practically move in these directions. How can we help each other in this process?

CHAPTER 3

There's a Storm Coming (The Tribulation)

The next major event in God's calendar is the Tribulation. Have you ever felt a storm coming? I grew up not far from the Gulf of Mexico in a town called Lake Charles, Louisiana. It was not uncommon for us to experience hurricanes during the rainy season. Even as I write this, New Orleans is recovering from the massive destruction of Hurricane Katrina and Lake Charles is without power after the beating it received from Hurricane Rita.

Such storms usually carried tell-tale signs that they were on the horizon. On a hot day, the wind would have hints of cold. The skies would darken, sometimes to the point of blackness. Streaks of brilliant lightning could be seen dancing across the distant sky, and thunder would rumble like a mighty dragon waking from a slumber. The waters in the bayou behind my house, and the big lake of Lake Charles itself, would begin to churn with activity. Something powerful and destructive was brewing. Would the levees hold?

Billy Graham, in his book, *Approaching Hoofbeats*, suggests that the signs of the times are pointing to the coming judgment of the world. Of the Prophet John and his stunning book of Revelation, Dr. Graham writes:

> "Very often I am inundated with the sounds of the city and of men and women in the city drowning themselves in activities and noise. I can stand on a corner in New York or Paris or London or Tokyo and I can see hopelessness, fear and boredom on the faces of hundreds. It would seem, on the surface, that John and I have almost nothing in common. Yet I can almost hear the voices he heard. I hear the approaching hoofbeats of the distant horsemen. I hear their warnings and, like John, I have no choice but to deliver them."

Indeed, the world does seem to be growing ever more dark. Sin is running rampant, war continues to shed blood at an alarming rate, and humanity is in pain. Even nature itself seems to be reeling from something, almost as if it senses danger and is barking out of control like the family dog upon seeing an intruder. Hurricanes, famines, forest fires, and a whole host of natural disasters are popping up all over the planet. Are these the signs that the end is near? Is The Storm on the horizon? I don't know about you, but I can feel the thunder.

Jesus helps us with this question. In Matthew 24, He gives specifics:

> *As Jesus was leaving the Temple grounds, his disci-*
> *ples pointed out to him the various Temple buildings.*
> *²But he told them, "Do you see all these buildings? I*
> *assure you, they will be so completely demolished that*
> *not one stone will be left on top of another!"*
>
> *³Later, Jesus sat on the slopes of the Mount of*
> *Olives. His disciples came to him privately and*
> *asked, "When will all this take place? And will there*

be any sign ahead of time to signal your return and the end of the world?"

⁴Jesus told them, "Don't let anyone mislead you. ⁵For many will come in my name, saying, 'I am the Messiah.' They will lead many astray. ⁶And wars will break out near and far, but don't panic. Yes, these things must come, but the end won't follow immediately. ⁷The nations and kingdoms will proclaim war against each other, and there will be famines and earthquakes in many parts of the world. ⁸But all this will be only the beginning of the horrors to come.

⁹"Then you will be arrested, persecuted, and killed. You will be hated all over the world because of your allegiance to me. ¹⁰And many will turn away from me and betray and hate each other. ¹¹And many false prophets will appear and will lead many people astray. ¹²Sin will be rampant everywhere, and the love of many will grow cold. ¹³But those who endure to the end will be saved. ¹⁴And the Good News about the Kingdom will be preached throughout the whole world, so that all nations will hear it; and then, finally, the end will come. Matthew 24:1-14 (NLT)

Notice that Jesus' disciples ask Him a specific question. They want to know what to look for as a signal of "the end of the world." Then Jesus gives a list of things that will happen before the judgment (oh, and by the way, the return of Jesus they're speaking of is the Second Coming, which we'll discuss later).

Signs that the end is near:

    a. Many False Messiahs. This has happened and continues to happen today. Several contemporary examples are Reverend Moon of the Moonies,

Charles Manson of Helter Skelter fame, and David Koresh of the Branch Davidians. All of these men claimed to be Jesus.

b. Massive Wars. Again, we've seen this in history and are currently in a war on terrorism.

c. Tremendous natural disasters. According to Georgia Tech's School of Earth and Science, the number of Category 4 and 5 hurricanes world-wide has nearly doubled over the past 35 years (*Science*, 9/16/05). The world has also experienced the recent destruction of a massive tsunami (precipitated by a 9.0 earthquake) and seen the Ethiopian famines of the 80's which, combined, killed over one million people (see CBC news online, 1/11/05). Evidence of the end? Only God knows. But it makes you think.

d. Horrible persecution of Christians. By some accounts, more persecution of Christians has happened in the 20th century than in any other time. Paul Marshall, in his book *Their Blood Cries Out*, reports that more than 200 million Christians are persecuted around the world in our time.

e. Rampant acceptance of sin and rebellion. This certainly characterizes my generation (Generation X! Rock on!).

f. The Gospel will be preached to all people groups. With the advent of technology, this is almost complete.

Certainly, there can be little doubt that the end of the world is moving closer. One could make an argument that most, if not all, of the signs have been completed and the earth is on the precipice of judgment.

The Tribulation: What, Who?

Before we move on, let's discuss the Tribulation in more detail. What is it? And who is it designed for?

What is the Tribulation?

The event known as the Tribulation is a seven-year period of judgment in which God unleashes a fury on the world, and particularly on the nation of Israel, unlike any disaster in history. The prophecies concerning it span both the Old and New Testaments. Let's take a quick survey of some key passages about this period:

When thou art in tribulation, and all these things are come upon thee, even in the latter days . . .
Deuteronomy 4:30 (KJV)

The earth has broken down and has utterly collapsed. Everything is lost, abandoned, and confused. ²⁰The earth staggers like a drunkard. It trembles like a tent in a storm. It falls and will not rise again, for its sins are very great.
²¹In that day the Lord will punish the fallen angels in the heavens and the proud rulers of the nations on earth. Isaiah 24:19-21 (NLT)

Alas, in all history when has there ever been a time of terror such as in that coming day? It is a time of trouble for my people—for Jacob—such as they have never known before. Yet God will rescue them! Jeremiah 30:7 (TLB)

This king will make a seven-year treaty with the people, but after half that time, he will break his pledge and stop the Jews from all their sacrifices and their offerings; then, as a climax to all his terrible deeds, the Enemy shall utterly defile the sanctuary of God. But in God's time and plan, his judgment will be poured out upon this Evil One." Daniel 9:27 (TLB)

Blow the trumpet in Jerusalem! Sound the alarm on my holy mountain! Let everyone tremble in fear because the day of the LORD is upon us. ²It is a day of darkness and gloom, a day of thick clouds and deep blackness. Suddenly, like dawn spreading across the mountains, a mighty army appears! How great and powerful they are! The likes of them have not been seen before and never will be seen again. Joel 2:1-2 (NLT)

"That terrible day of the LORD is near. Swiftly it comes—a day when strong men will cry bitterly. ¹⁵It is a day when the LORD'S anger will be poured out. It is a day of terrible distress and anguish, a day of ruin and desolation, a day of darkness and gloom, of clouds, blackness." Zephaniah 1:14-15 (NLT)

"The time will come when you will see what Daniel the prophet spoke about: the sacrilegious object that causes desecration standing in the holy place"— reader, pay attention! ¹⁶"Then those in Judea must flee to the hills. ¹⁷A person outside the house must not go inside to pack. ¹⁸A person in the field must not return even to get a coat. ¹⁹How terrible it will be for pregnant women and for mothers nursing their babies in those days. ²⁰And pray that your flight will not be in winter or on the Sabbath. ²¹For that will be a time of greater horror than anything the world has ever seen or will ever see again. ²²In fact, unless that time of calamity is shortened, the entire human race

*will be destroyed. But it will be shortened for the sake
of God's chosen ones. Matthew 24:15-22 (NLT)*

*Then the kings of the earth, the rulers, the generals,
the wealthy people, the people with great power, and
every slave and every free person—all hid themselves
in the caves and among the rocks of the mountains.*
*¹⁶And they cried to the mountains and the rocks,
"Fall on us and hide us from the face of the one who
sits on the throne and from the wrath of the Lamb.
¹⁷For the great day of their wrath has come, and who
will be able to survive?" Revelation 6:15-17 (NLT)*

This is just a brief survey of the Tribulation throughout
the Bible. Clearly, it's a terrible time of misery and wrath.
Notice that it's often referred to as a "day." The term "day"
in Scripture has a wide range of meanings. Obviously, in
certain contexts, it refers to a standard day. But, as Dr. John
Walvoord (prophecy expert extraordinaire) points out, in
biblical prophetic passages "day of the Lord" can have three
categories of meaning:

    A. Any period of time in the past or future when
       God deals directly in judgment on human sin.
    B. Specific future events constituting a judgment of
       God.
    C. A time in which God deals directly with the
       human situation, both in judgment and in
       blessing, hence broad enough to include not only
       the judgments preceding the Millennium but also
       the blessings of the Millennium itself (more on
       the Millennium, or 1000-Year Kingdom, later).

In the above passages, "day" clearly has the horrific
Tribulation judgment in view.

Dr. Dwight Pentecost, in his book *Things To Come,* notes some of the adjectives associated with this terrible day of the Lord: wrath, judgment, indignation, trial, trouble, destruction, darkness, desolations, overturning, and punishment. There can be no question that this will be the worst period the world has ever experienced.

Who is the Target of the Tribulation?

Notice in the above passages that there are three distinct groups in the Tribulation that can be classified as: Israel (Deut. 4:30; Jer. 30:7; Dan. 9:27; Joel 2:1-2), the World (Is. 24:19-21; Rev. 6:15-17), and the Chosen or the Elect (Mat. 24:15-22) . The Tribulation is designed primarily for the nation of Israel. God's goal in it is to move the nation to a broken place of humility in order that the Hebrews will finally recognize Christ as the Messiah. As in the past with Israel, God will use the time-tested method of judgment to bring about repentance. He will unleash Satan, the Antichrist, and the false prophet (the unholy trinity) on the planet just as He unleashed a demon on Saul in judgment (see 1 Sam. 16:14). God will also release an awful barrage of natural disasters on the planet. At the end of it all, Israel will be so broken that at least 144,000 biological Hebrews will accept Jesus as the Messiah and Israel will become a true Theocracy again with Christ as their King.

It is very important to recognize the decidedly Jewish nature of the Tribulation. Over and over again, the Scriptures clearly state that the primary purpose of this judgment is to turn the actual nation of Israel to Jesus. For example, the first reference to the Tribulation is Deuteronomy 4:29-30:

> *But if from there you seek the* LORD *your God, you will find him if you look for him with all your heart and with all your soul. ³⁰When you are in distress and all these things have happened to you, then in*

*later days you will return to the L*ORD *your God and
obey him. Deuteronomy 4:29-30 (NIV)*

Notice, first, that God is speaking to the people of Israel.
There is also a clear purpose to the "distress" (or tribula-
tion) they will experience: *"then . . . you will return to the
LORD your God and obey him."* The primary purpose of the
Tribulation is to turn Israel back to God.

Several other passages make it clear that this judgment is
intended primarily for this nation. Check out Jeremiah 30:7:

*In all history there has never been such a time of
terror. It will be a time of trouble for my people
Israel. Yet in the end, they will be saved! Jeremiah
30:7 (NLT)*

God is very clear in this passage. The Tribulation is described
as *"a time of trouble for my people Israel."* Repeatedly,
this period is connected directly and unquestionably to the
actual nation and people of Israel. God's goal is national
repentance.

Another group of people in the Tribulation is described
as "the World." This is the ungodly system of values, life-
style, and people we see at work throughout so much of our
world today. Therefore, a second purpose of this period is
to judge this pagan or unholy world system and its people.
Jesus refers to the Tribulation as the end of "the times of the
Gentiles" in Luke 21:24. The "times of the Gentiles" refers
to our current world order, which is increasingly running
away from God. Revelation 3:10 specifically identifies this
evil world order as a main object of God's fury when Jesus
states that His wrath is coming "upon all the world." There is
no question that all elements of this world which have turned
away from Christ and His ways will be judged severely
during this time.

A third group of people in the Tribulation is referred to as "the Chosen," "the Elect," or "Saints." These are people who experience the terror of the Tribulation and cry out to Christ in repentance. At least 144,000 of them are Israelites who will be kept alive through the period. Others will be people of other nations and races who accept Christ as their Savior and will be executed as a result. They will experience horrible persecution for their new-found faith at the hands of a world that violently opposes Christ.

Often, people confuse the Church with these people, so let me clarify a few issues. First, the terms "chosen," "elect," and "saint" can, indeed, refer to people in the Church today. However, the terms have a range of meaning and can refer to any follower of God during any age. In other words, these terms are not technical titles that refer to Church people alone. They can, and do, refer to any godly person of other ages. Also, there will be a "church" in the Tribulation that is not the true Church. As any pastor will tell you, many people in our congregations are not true followers of Jesus Christ and don't know Him as their Savior. As a matter of fact, there are entire churches and their pastors who don't know Him personally. These organizations, known by theologians collectively as "Christendom," will not be raptured. They'll continue to hold services and be religious in the name of Christ, even though they don't truly know Him. And there will be a form of "church worship" after the rapture, but it won't be founded on faith. Instead, it will be founded on empty ritual led by false teachers (see 1 Timothy 4:1-2 and 2 Timothy 3:1-5). Only the true Church, the body of true believers who really trust in Christ and have lives that evidence true belief, will be raptured.

Study Questions:

1. Look over the above passages and circle phrases that cause an emotional reaction in you. Share them with your group and how these phrases make you feel.

2. In light of the coming Tribulation, how do you now view Israel? How do you view the world? How will your view of these people move you to action?

3. What is something you can do this week to practically apply this lesson? Be specific.

CHAPTER 4

What Does "The Storm" Look Like? (The Early Years)

There are at least five prominent events that characterize this devastating period: The Antichrist's Treaty, The Antichrist's Abomination, Massive Judgments, The Battle of Armageddon, and The Resurrection of Old Testament and Tribulation Saints. In this chapter, we will examine the first two of the sequence in order to gain a better understanding of what the first half of the Tribulation will look like.

The Treaty and The Antichrist

Shortly after the rapture, the world will be thrown into terrible disarray. The sudden disappearance of every believer on the planet will cause cataclysmic chaos. Over a billion people claim to be Christians in the world today. Many of them are in crucial positions of power in every field of endeavor. Imagine a world instantly emptied of such a large percentage of godly people. When the terrorist attack of September 11, 2001 hit the United States, the shocking effects were immediate and worldwide. The stock market went into a spiral. The airline and travel industries suffered immensely. And international trade was massively handi-capped. America suffered huge economic losses that took years to recover. This event killed more than 3,000 people. Imagine millions and millions, all over the earth, gone "in the twinkling of an eye!" The world market will destabilize and disorder will run rampant. Such a context will be ripe for a strong, charismatic world leader to emerge and offer stability. That leader will be the Antichrist.

My first exposure to the concept of the "Antichrist" came from the movies, *The Omen* and *Damien Omen II*. Somehow, as a boy, I managed to sneak a peek at these movies against my parents' wishes, and the films terrified me! The Antichrist was presented as a little boy with a mark on his head that read "666" who was reluctant to embrace his demonic destiny. Eventually he turned murderous and accepted his identity as the future tyrant of the world. The films showed him having unlimited power with which he killed priests and other good people. The movies were bloody, with disgusting images of rabid dogs and grotesque murders. It seemed God's people had no strength against this coming monster. Was this portrayal accurate?

Scripture refers to the Antichrist as a powerful, attractive, skilled, and even supernatural international leader who is, indeed, terrifying. He will emerge from a ten-nation confed-eracy, probably in Europe. Eventually, he will be the leader of this "league of nations" and offer to stabilize the Middle East with a treaty of peace. His efforts will be noticed by the world and he will be given international acclaim. We read about him in Revelation 6:2:

I looked, and there before me was a white horse! Its rider held a bow, and he was given a crown, and he rode out as a conqueror bent on conquest. Revelation 6:2 (NIV)

Notice, the Antichrist is described as riding "a white horse." Jesus rides a white horse in Revelation 19. The Antichrist will resemble Christ and claim to be the Messiah. He will also appear to be a man of peace when he first gains prominence. In the image, he holds a bow without arrows. This may emphasize that he appears to be more of a diplomat than a warrior. Yet his ultimate goal, as the text says, is "conquest." He wants nothing less than to rule the world. And he will be given such a "crown" during the Tribulation. Take a look at the Prophet Daniel's vision of him in Daniel 7:7-8.

> *Then in my vision that night, I saw a fourth beast, terrifying, dreadful, and very strong. It devoured and crushed its victims with huge iron teeth and trampled what was left beneath its feet. It was different from any of the other beasts, and it had ten horns. ⁸As I was looking at the horns, suddenly another small horn appeared among them. Three of the first horns were wrenched out, roots and all, to make room for it. This little horn had eyes like human eyes and a mouth that was boasting arrogantly. Daniel 7:7-8 (NLT)*

Notice, Daniel refers to a "beast" that is incredibly powerful. This animal is described as having the ability to crush all those who get in its way. Notice also that this beast has "ten horns," three of which are viciously defeated by a "small horn" who has clearly positioned itself as the prominent horn. This little horn also has "human eyes" (perhaps indicating craftiness) and a very arrogant mouth.

At first, this seems like a dream John Lennon may have had back in the sixties! What in the wide, wide world of sports is going on here? Well, hang on, the dream gets interpreted for our terrified prophet by an angel. Check it out:

*I, Daniel, was troubled by all I had seen, and my
visions terrified me. [16]So I approached one of those
standing beside the throne and asked him what it all
meant. He explained it to me like this: [17]"These four
huge beasts represent four kingdoms that will arise
from the earth . . .*

*Then I wanted to know the true meaning of the
fourth beast, the one so different from the others and
so terrifying. It devoured and crushed its victims with
iron teeth and bronze claws, and it trampled what was
left beneath its feet. [20]I also asked about the ten horns
on the fourth beast's head and the little horn that came
up afterward and destroyed three of the other horns.
This was the horn that seemed greater than the others
and had human eyes and a mouth that was boasting
arrogantly. Daniel 7:15-17, 19-20 (NLT)*

*"This fourth animal," he told me, "is the fourth
world power that will rule the earth. It will be more
brutal than any of the others; it will devour the whole
world, destroying everything before it. [24]His ten
horns are ten kings that will rise out of his empire;
then another king will arise, more brutal than the
other ten, and will destroy three of them. [25]He will
defy the Most High God and wear down the saints
with persecution, and he will try to change all laws,
morals, and customs. God's people will be helpless
in his hands for three and a half years. Daniel 7:23-
25 (TLB)*

Several things are clear from this prophecy. The Antichrist
will come from an extremely powerful empire that appears
to be a confederation of ten national leaders representing ten
nations. In a move for power, this national leader will destroy
three of the original ten and consolidate his rule over all the
other kingdoms. His tactics will also be brutal and totalitarian

in nature. And his empire will be staggering in terms of its destructive capacity. Oh, and by the way, many scholars believe this empire is a confederation of European countries because when the same group is mentioned in the book of Revelation, we're told that its primary location is in a place with "seven hills" (see Rev. 17:9). One location that was known prominently in the ancient world as a land of seven hills was Rome. Also, Daniel describes the Antichrist as having come from the same people who destroyed the temple in Jerusalem in the first century—that is, the Roman Empire (see Dan. 9:26). So, there is solid evidence to believe the Antichrist will lead a revived Roman Empire in the final days.

With this empire in hand, he will devise an ingenious treaty that finally seems to solve all the tensions of the Middle East. Can you imagine such a thing today? All my life there has been trouble in the Middle East. It seems like every day since I was a boy watching the news on my father's lap, some kind of treaty has been violated or some violence has broken out between the Arabs and the Israelis. The Holy Land has been an area of constant friction and hatred for as long as I can remember! However, at some point in the future, a world leader will rise to prominence and broker a peace treaty in this region that appears to be air-tight. Peace will seem to finally come to the Middle East and the Antichrist will be lauded as a political genius. Take a look at Daniel 9:27:

> *This king will make a seven-year treaty with the people, but after half that time, he will break his pledge and stop the Jews from all their sacrifices and their offerings; then, as a climax to all his terrible deeds, the Enemy shall utterly defile the sanctuary of God. But in God's time and plan, his judgment will be poured out upon this Evil One." Daniel 9:27 (TLB)*

This passage foresees an alarming development. The Antichrist will make a treaty with Israel for seven years, but in "half that time" he will betray the Jews and assert hideous control not only over their government, but over their religious practices as well. Note, this "Enemy shall utterly defile the sanctuary of God." This is known as the "Abomination of Desolation."

The Antichrist's Abomination

Up to this point, the Antichrist has provided stability to the world after the rapture. He has consolidated power in Europe and given peace to the Middle East. Now, with his power complete, he takes a horrific turn. In a shocking act of sacrilege, he sets himself up as God in Jerusalem and demands worship. The prophet John describes what Daniel saw in Revelation 13:11-18:

Then I saw another beast come up out of the earth. He had two horns like those of a lamb, and he spoke with the voice of a dragon. [12]He exercised all the authority of the first beast. And he required all the earth and those who belong to this world to worship the first beast, whose death-wound had been healed. [13]He did astounding miracles, such as making fire flash down to earth from heaven while everyone was watching. [14]And with all the miracles he was allowed to perform on behalf of the first beast, he deceived all the people who belong to this world. He ordered the people of the world to make a great statue of the first beast, who was fatally wounded and then came back to life. [15]He was permitted to give life to this statue so that it could speak. Then the statue commanded that anyone refusing to worship it must die.

[16]He required everyone—great and small, rich and poor, slave and free—to be given a mark on the right hand or on the forehead. [17]And no one could buy or sell anything without that mark, which was either the name of the beast

*or the number representing his name. ¹⁸Wisdom is needed
to understand this. Let the one who has understanding solve
the number of the beast, for it is the number of a man. His
number is 666. Revelation 13:11-18 (NLT)*

There is a lot in this passage, and I won't attempt to hit
everything. But I will point out some shocking highlights
(or, should I say, lowlights). First, notice there is an "unholy
trinity" at work here. We have the first "beast" (or, as Daniel
calls him, the "little horn"). Then we have "another beast."
And, finally, we have the "dragon." These images refer to the
Antichrist, the False Prophet, and Satan himself respectively.
Here's how I break these three down in my mind. Satan is
clearly in charge as the unholy "father." The Antichrist is a
very gifted man who has obviously given his life to Satan,
has been possessed by the Evil One, and has been given
supernatural ability. He claims, at this point, to be Christ the
Son. One way he does this is to imitate the resurrection (see
the end of v. 14). The vast majority of the world believes
him and accepts him not only as their "World King," but
also as the Messiah Himself. His "Secretary of State" and
"Archbishop" is the second beast who is a false prophet. He,
too, is given considerable authority from Satan and has supernatural ability. He can, for example, force people to worship
the Antichrist and is able to call fire down from heaven (not
unlike God's true prophets in the Old Testament!).

Three and a half years after the Israeli Peace Treaty, this
ungodly trinity sets up headquarters in Jerusalem, erects
an idol to the Antichrist in the Temple (which, by the way,
will be rebuilt by that time) demands global worship of the
idol, and exerts tyrannical power on the planet. People will
not even be able to purchase food without bowing to the
Antichrist and having his mark placed on their body as a sort
of imbedded credit card. Judgment has come, and it comes
with fury.

Study Questions:

1. In addition to the passages cited above, read the following concerning the Antichrist:

   Daniel 11:36-46; 2 Thessalonians 2:3-10; Revelation 17:8-14

   Describe how you picture him. Is there a television or movie character that reminds you of him and why?

   Why do you think he doesn't have more power now (hint, 2 Thes. 2:3-10)? If he is in power already, how do you think you could recognize him?

2. The Bible teaches that we are a temple for the Holy Spirit (see 1 Corinthians 6:9-20). How do you think we sometimes can desecrate our temples before God?

3. Break up into pairs and, if the Spirit leads, confess any sin that's prevalent in your life and pray for one another (see James 5:16). This is God's way to clean His temple.

CHAPTER 5

What Does "The Storm" Look Like? (The Great Tribulation)

The second half of the Tribulation is a terrifying mixture of global war, extreme tragedy, and wide-spread pain. These three and a half years, which begin with the Abomination, are known as "The Great Tribulation" and far surpass any devastation in the history of the world. For our purposes, we will examine three deadly cycles that gain great momentum as soon as the Temple is desecrated: The Judgments.

The Judgments

The book of Revelation, chapters 6-16, describes massive judgments that will shake the world during the Great Tribulation. These judgments come in three sets of seven catastrophic events each. They also increase in intensity as they progress. The first set of seven is the Seal Judgments.

The Seal Judgments

John the Prophet is shown a future in which Jesus opens seven seals. Each seal represents a judgment that's coming. I picture this sort of like a book of matches. Jesus picks up the first match and strikes it. The first then spreads to the second, and the third, and so on. The fire then spreads to the table the matches are on, then on to the room, the mansion, the neighborhood . . . well, you get the picture. The first seal is the Antichrist himself. While he doesn't know it, he has been ordained to ascend in power as an agent of God's wrath. Take a look at Revelation 6:1-2:

> *As I watched, the Lamb broke the first of the seven seals on the scroll. Then one of the four living beings called out with a voice that sounded like thunder, "Come!" [2]I looked up and saw a white horse. Its rider carried a bow, and a crown was placed on his head. He rode out to win many battles and gain the victory. Rev. 6:1-2 (NLT)*

The world has an evil tyrant unleashed on her. All hell breaks loose soon after. It should be noted that this may refer to the beginning of the Tribulation. The first four seals appear to occur during the time of relative peace three and a half years before the Abomination. Then, when the fifth seal is opened, we have the Great Tribulation. The fire spreads to an inferno!

The second through fourth seals represent warfare (possibly the warfare that gives the Antichrist his position of power over the ten-nation confederacy), famine with very high inflation, and widespread death. All of these are conditions favorable for an assertive world leader to rise in prominence. It should be noted that at this point, a quarter of the earth has been killed by warfare, famine, plague, and animals (see Rev. 6:7-8). And God is just getting started.

The fifth through seventh seals get more intense. The Antichrist has seized global power and has an invincible army. In his hatred, he unleashes a furious persecution on anyone who has accepted Christ as Lord since the rapture. The name of Jesus will be abhorred during this time and anyone showing allegiance to the true God will be summarily executed (Rev. 6:9-11). The sixth seal unleashes cosmic catastrophies unrivaled even in a Hollywood epic. Among these events are a huge earthquake, meteor showers, and mountains literally crumbling to the ground (Rev. 6:12-17). And we're not even done with the first set! The final seal opens the second set of judgments, the Trumpet Judgments.

The Trumpet Judgments

The Trumpet Judgments are even faster and more devastating than the Seal Judgments! They begin with five catastrophic natural disasters. The first trumpet blows and one third of the earth is scorched by flaming hail (Rev. 8:7). Following this horror, a third of the sea dies and a third of all ships in the world are destroyed. This happens as a result of the second trumpet when a large, inflamed mountain hits the oceans (Rev. 8:8-9). The third trumpet causes one third of the rivers in the world to be polluted beyond use (Rev. 8:10-11). The fourth trumpet darkens the sky to be followed by a hellish locust plague with the fifth trumpet (Rev. 8:12-9:12). When the sixth trumpet blows, this series of judgments ends with a massive and bloodthirsty army of over two hundred million soldiers riding on fire-breathing horses, massacring millions (Rev. 9:13-21). Then the seventh trumpet sounds, which starts the Bowl Judgments.

It's interesting to note that all these images are being viewed by John the Prophet, a first century man using first century descriptions. Hal Lindsey, in his book *The Late Great Planet Earth*, suggests that all of these plagues are consistent with modern warfare. For example, flaming hail could describe missiles. A mountain on fire could be describing a nuclear warhead which would darken the sun and pollute water supplies by its radioactive fallout. The locust plague could very well be combat helicopters dispersing nerve gas. Certainly, current weapons of warfare fit these descriptions.

The Bowl Judgments

With each wave of judgment, the world suffers even greater agony. The Bowl Judgments begin with a plague of painful, ugly sores (perhaps from radiation poisoning) (Rev. 16:1-2). The second and third bowls destroy the sea and all remaining rivers. No fresh water can be found (Rev. 16:3-7). The sun begins to scorch the survivors, but over the beast there is complete darkness as the fourth and fifth bowls are poured out (Rev. 16:8-11). The Battle of Armageddon draws near as the Euphrates River dries up, eliminating it as a natural barrier and allowing troops from the East to cross with the sixth bowl (Rev. 16:12-16). And finally, a more devastating earthquake than any before takes place with unprecedented natural catastrophes accompanying it. The destruction is so violent that Jerusalem is literally broken into three pieces and mountains collapse the world over (Rev. 16:17-21). The earth has literally been beaten to a pulp, and humanity is in shambles.

Study Questions:

1. Break your Small Group up into three divisions. Assign one group the Seal Judgments (Rev. 6), one the Trumpet Judgments (Rev. 8-9), and one the Bowl Judgments (Rev. 15-16). Try to imagine what modern tragedies may look like to John and share what you think he may be seeing (i.e. locusts may be helicopters).

2. Read aloud as a group Revelation 9:20-21. What
   strikes you about these people who are the objects of
   God's wrath?

3. How does this affect your efforts to reach people for Christ?

CHAPTER 6

The Second Coming,
The Millennial Kingdom, and
The Final State

Most Christians have memorized the Lord's Prayer at one time or another. I learned it back in the days when everyone said it at the end of football games. I have vivid memories of kneeling with my teammates on the fifty yard line and giving God honor through those hallowed words. It begins with, "Our Father, who art in Heaven, Hallowed be Thy Name, Thy Kingdom come, Thy will be done, on earth as it is in Heaven." The Second Coming is the ultimate answer to that prayer. Earth will manifest God's will just as it is manifested in Heaven on the day Christ comes back in glory. In this chapter we will see three wonderful hopes associated with this tremendous event and briefly examine the Millennial Kingdom along with the Final State of the world.

Three Wonderful Hopes of the Second Coming:

1. The Second Coming will fulfill Christ's Word.

Immediately after Jesus ascends, His disciples stand frozen with their mouths gaping wide open as they stare at the location in the sky where a portal has just transported Jesus into the dimension of Heaven. Suddenly, two angels approach them and make a promise. Take a look:

> As they were straining their eyes to see him, two white-robed men suddenly stood there among them. *11They* said, "Men of Galilee, why are you standing here staring at the sky? Jesus has been taken away from you into heaven. And someday, just as you saw him go, he will return!" Acts 1:10-11 (NLT)

We're promised that Jesus will return one day in glory. He will reappear in the sky and descend to our planet to take over. Jesus Himself promised this in Matthew 25:

> "But when the Son of Man comes in his glory, and all the angels with him, then he will sit upon his glorious throne. *32All* the nations will be gathered in his presence, and he will separate them as a shepherd separates the sheep from the goats. *33He* will place the sheep at his right hand and the goats at his left. Matthew 25:31-33 (NLT)

Make no mistake about it, Jesus is coming back. At that time, the awesome cycle of judgments will have left the world angry and Satan even more rebellious than ever. The armies of the world will declare war on Christ with an intense hatred. They may actually believe they have a chance against the King of Kings because of the rule of evil during the Tribulation. They will be sorely mistaken.

2. The Second Coming will correct all that's wrong with the world.

As these wicked armies array themselves for battle against the King of Kings at the plains of Armageddon (this is an actual plain outside of Israel, see Rev. 16:14), Christ will rout them with very little effort. Let's take a peek in Revelation 19:

> *Then I saw heaven opened, and a white horse was standing there. And the one sitting on the horse was named Faithful and True. For he judges fairly and then goes to war.* *¹²His eyes were bright like flames of fire, and on his head were many crowns. A name was written on him, and only he knew what it meant.* *¹³He was clothed with a robe dipped in blood, and his title was the Word of God.* *¹⁴The armies of heaven, dressed in pure white linen, followed him on white horses.* *¹⁵From his mouth came a sharp sword, and with it he struck down the nations. He ruled them with an iron rod, and he trod the winepress of the fierce wrath of almighty God.* *¹⁶On his robe and thigh was written this title: King of kings and Lord of lords. Revelation 19:11-16 (NLT)*

I love this passage! Read it again and let it sink in. This is where we're headed as the people of God! Notice that Jesus comes with an army that's "dressed in pure white linen." Do you know who that is? That's me and you, if you're a follower of Christ! These are the redeemed of the ages, and everything wrong that's ever been done to us, or that we've done wrong to others, has been fixed! We're pure! No more sin. No more pain. No more sorrow. Life is perfect for us! And guess what we get to do when Jesus comes back and faces these evil forces? We get to watch Him kick their tails! Look at what happens in v. 15. A "sharp sword" comes out of His mouth and His enemies are struck down. In Scripture, the sword is a picture of the "Word of God" (see Eph. 6:17). Jesus is so dominant that He only has to say a word and literally millions and millions and millions of His enemies are wiped out! He truly is the King of kings and Lord of lords!

3. The Second Coming will emphatically demonstrate that Satan is no match for God.

All of us have been hurt by evil in our lives. We've lost battles against temptation, and we've been the object of someone else's temptation. Some of us have heard the cruel laughter of Satan in abuse or neglect. There's no question about it—Satan has hurt us all. But the story isn't over. One day, Satan will be utterly humiliated by our Lord. Revelation 19:20-20:2 gives us a preview:

> *And the beast was captured, and with him the false prophet who did mighty miracles on behalf of the beast—miracles that deceived all who had accepted the mark of the beast and who worshiped his statue. Both the beast and his false prophet were thrown alive into the lake of fire that burns with sulfur. 21Their entire army was killed by the sharp sword that came out of the mouth of the one riding the white horse. And all the vultures of the sky gorged themselves on the dead bodies.*
>
> *20:1Then I saw an angel come down from heaven with the key to the bottomless pit and a heavy chain in his hand. 2He seized the dragon—that old serpent, the Devil, Satan—and bound him in chains for a thousand years. Revelation 19:20-20:2 (NLT)*

There are three places of torment and punishment referred to in Scripture: Hades, the Abyss, and Hell. Hades is a very unpleasant holding cell for those awaiting final judgment at the Great White Throne Judgment. The Abyss is a spiritual dungeon where demonic forces are held prisoner. And Hell proper is a fiery place that stinks terribly and produces constant torment. In this passage, the Antichrist and his False Prophet are thrown alive into Hell. Then Satan is bound in the Abyss by the Archangel Michael. I find it interesting that Jesus doesn't bind Satan Himself. It's as if Satan is no threat at all to Christ, which is certainly the case. Jesus can delegate Satan's imprisonment to an angel!

The Millennial Kingdom (The 1000-Year Kingdom)

I want to close with a few words about the earthly reign of Christ from this point on. Once Christ completes this wonderful display of His power, He will literally rule the earth for a thousand years. This is known as the Millennial Kingdom, and it will be populated by those who survive the Tribulation (at least 144,000 of which will be believing Israelites—see Rev. 7:4). The world will experience a time of peace and tranquility such as it has never known. And all of the prophetic promises made in the Old Testament to Israel concerning an eternal kingdom and extended borders will be fulfilled.

At the end of this reign, Satan will be released to tempt the world one last time and will manage to muster up another massive rebellion. Once again, the armies of the world will try to defeat Christ. Yet this time, fire from heaven will destroy them and Satan will be thrown into Hell once and for all (see Rev. 20).

Jesus will then open up His record books and judge all those in Hades awaiting their fate. Undoubtedly tyrants like Hitler and murderers like Jack the Ripper will be counted among them. Each will stand before the Judge's throne, a Great White Throne, and be sentenced. This will constitute the final judgment of the dead, and death will no longer exist after this (Rev. 20:11-15).

The Final State

I like stories with happy endings. As a matter of fact, I won't read a book if I know it ends badly or will make me depressed when I've finished it. That's why I'm so encouraged by what I see in God's prophecies. History has a happy ending! After the Great White Throne Judgment, the dimension of Heaven will take over our reality. There will literally be a new Heaven and a new earth. The Heavenly Jerusalem will descend like a breathtaking, sculpted city of art onto a newly re-created earth. All tears will be wiped away and *"there will be no more death or mourning or crying or pain, for the old order of things has passed away." (Rev. 21:4).*

One of the awesome things I know about my precious Savior is that He makes things new. All of history reminds me that He is great and humanity isn't great without Him. I'm so thankful He has remade me in so many ways and saved me from a life dominated by sin. And I praise Him for the absolute fact that in the end all believers, and the earth itself, will be re-created for His great glory. My favorite quote of all biblical prophecies is a fitting promise on which to close. If you're struggling with an injustice, if you've been hurt to the point of despair, if you've lost hope, soak up this verse and memorize it. God has a promise for you:

And he that sat upon the throne said, "Behold, I make all things new." And he said unto me, "Write: for these words are true and faithful" (emphasis mine). *Revelation 21:5 (KJV)*

Study Questions:

1. Read chapters 20-22 of Revelation and try to draw a rough sketch of what the Heavenly Jerusalem looks like.

2. Do you have anything you're hoping to see made right by the Lord in your life (any pain, mistake, or injustice committed against you)? If you're comfortable, share it with the group.

3. Spend a time of prayer thanking God specifically about things you've learned in this study.

Bibliography

Books

Graham, Billy. *Approaching Hoofbeats.* Waco: Word, 1983.

Lindsey, Hal. *There's a New World Coming.* Irvine, CA: Harvest House, 1973.

Pentecost, J. Dwight. *Things to Come.* Grand Rapids: Academie Books, 1964.

Ryrie, Charles C. *Dispensationalism Today.* Chicago: Moody, 1965.

Walvoord, John F. and Roy B. Zuck, Ed.s. *The Bible Knowledge Commentary.* Victor Books, 1988.

Walvoord, John F. *The Rapture Question.* Grand Rapids: Academie Books, 1979.

Walvoord, John F. *Prophecy.* Nashville: Thomas Nelson, 1993.

Wiersbe, Warren W. *The Bible Exposition Commentary.* Vol. 2. Colorado Springs: Chariot Victor Publishing, 1989.

Appendix

The following sermon is one of the few remaining from my great grandfather, Samuel R. Henderson. Rev. Henderson was an itinerate preacher in the early 1900's who was a noted teacher on end times throughout southern Louisiana. This sermon covers the Palestinian Covenant, which was given by the Lord to Israel during the Age of Law. It reaffirmed and enlarged the original Abrahamic Covenant with specific references to the promises of land to an actual nation of Israel.

There are two good reasons to include it. First, it addresses the future of the Jewish people in the Age of the Future Kingdom. Again, Scripture gives tangible promises of real events in the history of Israel. God is not done with His chosen people as a distinct entity from the Church.

The sermon also shows the continuity of theological insight and revelation from generation to generation. My great grandfather preached this message years before Israel was reconstituted as a nation in 1948. Israel as we know it today did not even exist! Yet God's people were predicting, against all evidence, that God would begin to gather Jews from all over the world into a national entity again in Palestine. Rev. Henderson trusted God's Word to be fulfilled. And, today, before our very eyes, the beginnings of the Palestinian Covenant have taken clear shape. The Bible and its truth transcend every generation. It has stood and will stand the test of time. Thank God we have such a precious gift!

THE PALESTINIAN COVENANT

COMPILED BY

S.R. HENDERSON

Iota, Louisiana

INTRODUCTION

This is the second of a series of messages on the end of this age, and the coming of Jesus and the establishing of His Kingdom on earth. Some of the truths contained in these messages are startling in their simplicity, and also it is rather remarkable that, while they are *so clearly taught* in the Word of God, they have been overlooked or neglected by the great majority of God's people. This may be accounted for by keeping in mind that God reveals the truth at such time as it is needed. It is also significant that in the past few months these same truths are being looked into by many of the ministers of all faiths — Protestant — Catholic, and Jew. We are in the time of the end — the night is far spent — the day is at hand — let us put off the works of darkness and put on the armour of light.

THE PALESTINIAN
COVENANT

S ome four hundred years after God had appeared to
Abraham and given him the land of Palestine as an ever-
lasting possession, He affirmed His promise to the children
of Israel with conditions. He gave more of the details and
explained more fully as to the future of His chosen people.
In Deuteronomy 28:63-67 we read: "And it shall come to
pass, that as the Lord rejoiced over you to do you good, and
to multiply you; so the Lord will rejoice over you to destroy
you, and to bring you to nought; and ye shall be plucked
from off the land whither thou goest to possess it. And the
Lord shall scatter thee among all people, from the one end
of the earth even unto the other; and there thou shalt serve
other gods, which neither thou nor thy fathers have known,
even wood and stone. And among these nations shalt thou
find no ease, neither shall the sole of thy foot have rest: but
the Lord shall give thee there a trembling heart, and a failing
of eyes, and sorrow of mind: and thy life shall hang in doubt
before thee; and thou shalt fear day and night, and shall have
none assurance of thy life; in the morning thou shalt say,
Would God it were even! and at even thou shalt say, Would

God it were morning! for the fear of thine heart wherewith thou shalt fear, and for the sight of thine eyes which thou shalt see."

Not only was a curse to come upon the children of Israel for their disobedience, but in Deuteronomy 39:22-23 we find that a curse was to be put also upon the land of Palestine. In verses 24-28 we read, "Even all nations shall say, Wherefore hath the Lord done thus unto this land? What meaneth the heat of this great anger? Men shall say, Because they have forsaken the covenant of the Lord God of their fathers, which He made with them when He brought them forth out of the land of Egypt: for they went and served other gods, and worshipped them, gods whom they knew not, and whom He had not given unto them: and the anger of the Lord was kindled against this land, to bring upon it all the curses that are written in this book: and the Lord rooted them out of their land in anger, and in wrath, and in great indignation, and cast them into another land, as it is this day." We can clearly see that these scriptures do not refer to the Babylonish Captivity which was of only seventy years duration but to the final dispersion of A. D. 70. How literally these prophecies have been fulfilled. For many centuries the land of Palestine has been in desolation and the children of Abraham, strangers, scattered over all the face of the earth. No one can deny that these were literal prophecies and that they have been fulfilled literally and not just spiritually or figuratively.

Now in Deuteronomy 30:1-9 we have the Palestinian Covenant clearly stated; and we must remember that it is also literal and must be literally fulfilled. "And it shall come to pass, when all these things are come upon thee, the blessing and the curse, which I have set before thee, and thou shalt call them to mind among all the nations, whither the Lord thy God hath driven thee, (this is being fulfilled at this present time,) and shalt return unto the Lord thy God, and shalt obey His voice according to all that I command thee this day, thou and thy children, with all thine heart, and with all thy soul; (because of their terrible afflictions and sorrows, the Jews throughout the world are praying and seeking the face of their God as never before, perhaps in all their history,) that then the Lord thy God *will turn thy captivity, and have compassion upon thee, and will return and gather thee from all the nations, whither the Lord thy God hath scattered thee.* If any of thine be driven out unto the utmost parts of heaven, from thence will the Lord thy God gather thee, and from thence will He fetch thee: and the Lord thy God will bring thee into the land which thy fathers possessed, and thou shalt possess it; and He will do thee good, and multiply thee above thy fathers. And the Lord thy God will circumcise thine heart, and the heart of thy seed, to love the Lord thy God with all thine heart, and with all thy soul, that thou mayest live. And the Lord thy God will put all these curses upon thine enemies, and on them that hate thee, which persecuteth thee. And thou shalt return and obey the voice of the Lord, and do all His commandments which I command thee this day. And the Lord thy God will make thee plenteous in every work of thine hand, in the fruit of thy body, and in the fruit of thy cattle, and in the fruit of thy land, for good: for the Lord will again rejoice over thee for good, as He rejoiced over thy fathers."

This is not a mere spiritual prophecy but is a plain positive promise that when Israel shall have been scattered over all the earth and are in sorrow and distress for their disobedience to God, and shall repent and turn to God, that He will have mercy upon them and shall turn again to them and bring them back to the land of Palestine, and will bless them and prosper them both in the labor of their hands, and the fruit of their body. Children will be born to them, and they will again have herds of cattle. Many reject this prophecy as being literal because it does not fit in with their preconceived ideas and traditions. Some think this only has reference to the pouring out of the Holy Ghost and the calling of the Gentiles. This does violence to every method of interpretation of prophecy. A careful consideration of this prophecy will show the foolishness of this idea.

The Palestinian Covenant is clearly set forth in the following order: dispersion for disobedience, future repentance, God hears and turns again to Israel, restoration to the land of Palestine, national conversion (a nation born in a day,) judgments on the oppressors of Israel, and for Israel prosperity and blessedness. Saint Paul gives a very clear exposition of the restoration of Israel in Romans II, "I say then, hath God cast away His people? God forbid. For I also am an Israelite, of the seed of Abraham, of the tribe of Benjamin. God hath not cast away His people (Israel) which He foreknew. Wot ye not what the scriptures saith of Elias? How he maketh intercession to God against Israel saying, "Lord they have killed thy prophets, and digged down thine altars; and I am left alone and they seek my life." But what saith the answer of God unto him? I have reserved to myself seven thousand men who have not bowed the knee to Baal. Even so, then at the present time also there is a remnant according to the election of grace. And if by grace, then is it no more of works, otherwise grace is no more grace. But if it be of works, then is it no more grace: otherwise work is no more work. What then? Israel hath not obtained that which be seeketh for; but the election hath obtained it, and the rest were blinded (according as it is written, God hath given them the spirit of slumber, eyes that they should not see, and ears that they should not hear;) unto this day. And David saith, "Let their table be made a snare, and a trap, and a stumbling block, and a recompence unto them; let their eyes be darkened, that they may not see, and bow down their back alway." I say then, "Have they stumbled that they should fall? God forbid: but rather through their fall salvation has come unto the Gentiles, for to provoke them (the Israelites) to jealousy. Now if the fall of them be the riches of the world, and the diminishing of them the riches of the Gentiles; how much more their fulness? For I speak to you Gentiles, inasmuch as I am the apostle of the Gentiles. I magnify mine office: if by any means I may provoke to emulation them which are my flesh, and might save some of them. For if the casting away of them be the reconciling of the world, what shall the receiving of them be, but life from the dead? For if the first fruit be holy, the lump is also holy: and if the root he holy, so are the branches. And if some of the branches being broken off, and thou, being a wild olive tree, (the Gentiles), wert grafted in among them (the Israelites,) and with them partakest of the root and fatness of the olive tree; boast not against the branches (the part of Israel that was broken off.) But if thou boast, thou bearest not the root, but the root thee. Thou wilt say then, "The branches were broken off, that I might be grafted in." Well; because of unbelief they were broken off, and thou standest by faith. Be not high minded but fear: for if God spared not the natural branches, take heed lest He also spare not thee. Behold therefore the goodness and severity of God: on them which fell, severity; but toward thee, goodness, if thou continue in His goodness: otherwise thou shalt be cut off (this is what happens at the end of the Gentile age.) And they also (Israel,) if they abide not still in unbelief (they are now repenting and calling on God for mercy,) shall be grafted in (this is soon to take place;) for God is able to graft them in again. For if thou (the Gentile church who have become, by faith, the children of Abraham) wert cut out of the olive tree which is wild by nature (being aliens from the commonwealth of Israel, Ephesians 2:12,) and wert grafted contrary to nature into a good olive tree: how much more shall these, which be the natural branches, be grafted into their own olive tree? For I would not brethren, that you should be ignorant of this mystery, lest ye should be wise in your own conceits; that blindness in part has happened to Israel, until the fulness of the Gentiles be come in (the end of the

Gentile age.) And so all Israel shall be saved: as it is written, "There shall come out of Sion the Deliverer, and shall turn away ungodliness from Jacob (something not yet fulfilled:) for this is my covenant unto them, when I shall take away their sins. As concerning the gospel, they are enemies for your sake: but as touching the election, they are beloved for the fathers' sake. For the gifts and calling of God are without repentance. For as ye in times past have not believed God, yet have now obtained mercy through their unbelief: even so have these also not believed, that through your mercy they also may obtain mercy. For God hath concluded them all in unbelief, that He might have mercy upon all."

This chapter sets forth clearly the following truths: that a remnant would be saved from among the Israelites during the church age, that there had always been a remnant, as in Elijah's time, the national unbelief in Jesus' day, the turning of God unto the Gentiles, the breaking off of some of the branches, the Gentile church being grafted in, Israel being grafted in (nationally,) the coming of the Deliverer who shall restore them. There is no scripture that teaches that the Gentile church now enjoys or inherits the literal promises made to the Israelites; but it does enjoy the spiritual blessings and shall be partakers jointly with literal Israel to the blessings of the restored kingdom of Israel which is to be the highest and most exalted state yet enjoyed by man since the fall of Adam.

In Acts 15:14-18, "Simeon hath declared how God at the first did visit the Gentiles to take out of them a people for His name. And to this agree the words of the prophets, as it is written. After this I will return and will build again the tabernacle of David which is fallen down, and I will build again the ruins thereof and I will set it up, that the residue of men might seek after the Lord and all the Gentiles upon whom my name is called saith the Lord who doeth all these things. Known unto the Lord are all His works from the beginning of the world." This is one of the most important passages in the New Testament. It sets forth in a very few words the divine purpose for this age or dispensation and also for the beginning of the next, or the Kingdom Age. First, there is the taking out from among the Gentiles a people for His name, the Gentile Church, the called out ones, or Ecclesia. "After this," that is after the calling out of the church, "I will return." This quotation is from Amos 9:11-12. Let us read it. "In that day will I raise up the tabernacle of David that is fallen, and close up the breaches thereof; and I will raise up his ruins, and I will build it as in the days of old: (as in David's day -- a literal rebuilding:) (that they may possess the remnant of Edom, and of all the heathen, which are called by my name, saith the Lord that doeth this." Continuing, we read, "Behold, the days come, saith the Lord, that the plowman shall overtake the reaper, and the trader of grapes him that soweth seed; and the mountains shall drop sweet wine, and all the hills shall melt. And I will bring again the captivity of my people of Israel, and they shall build the waste cities, and inhabit them; and they shall plant vineyards, and drink the wine thereof; they shall also make gardens, and eat the fruit of them. And I will plant them upon their land, and they shall no more be pulled out of their land which I have given them, saith the Lord thy God."

These prophecies cannot be spiritualized or set aside. They are in perfect harmony with the Palestinian Covenant. God's chosen people, the Israelites, are to be restored to the land of their fathers. They are to he wonderfully blessed of God. The Deliverer, who is Jesus of Nazareth, shall return to be their King. What our opinion might be is of no conse-quence. God's Word must be fulfilled. If one part fails, then it all fails. No chain is stronger than its weakest link. If the promise made to the Israelites fail, then the promises to the Gentiles shall also fail.

Turning to Ezekiel 20 and beginning at the 34th verse, we read, "And I will bring you out from the people, and will gather you out of the countries wherein ye are scattered, with a mighty hand, and with a stretched out arm, and with fury poured out. And I will bring you into the wilderness of the people, and there will I plead with you face to face. Like as I pleaded with your fathers in the wilderness of the land of Egypt, so will I plead with you, saith the Lord God. And I will cause you to pass under the rod, and I will bring you into the bond of the covenant: and I will purge out from among you the rebels, and them that transgress against me: I will bring them forth out of the country where they sojourn, and they shall not enter into the land of Israel: and ye shall know that I am the Lord. As for you, O house of Israel, thus saith the Lord God; Go ye, serve ye every one his idols, and hereafter also, if ye will not harken unto me but pollute ye my holy name no more with your gifts, and with idols. For in mine holy mountain, in the month of the height of Israel, saith the Lord God, there shall all the house of Israel, all of them in the land, serve me: there will I accept them, and there will I require your offerings, and the firstfruits of your oblations, with all your holy things. I will accept you with your sweet savour, when I bring you out from the people, and gather you out of the countries wherein ye have been scattered; and I will be sanctified in you before the heathen. And ye shall know that I am the Lord, when I shall bring you into the land of Israel, into the country for the which I lifted up mine hand to give it to your fathers."

These scriptures are so plain and emphatic that they need no explanation. Surely, God will do what be has promised. There is no question that these scriptures have not been fulfilled in the past. They are yet future.

In I Corinthians 15:8, Paul referred to himself as one born out of due time or as the Greek implies, before the time.

He was here looking forward to the future national conversion of Israel.

Today we have trouble and distress in all nations and perplexity, The nations of the world are on the brink of an awful precipice, with no hope of averting certain disaster.

Our civilization is doomed. Governments are tottering and kingdoms crumbling. But the people of God can, by faith, see beyond the darkness and the gathering clouds, beyond the sufferings and persecutions, beyond the sighings and tears to the glorious light of the eternal day, when the darkness shall be dispelled, and Jesus Christ, the King eternal, the King of Kings and Lord of Lords, shall come bringing deliverance and peace. Then sorrow and sighing shall flee away, and God Himself shall wipe all tears from our eyes.

(Be sure to read the next message, The Palestinian Covenant.)

I have made arrangements with the printer to publish, one at a time. There will be approximately twelve messages in the series; if you have a desire to inform yourself concerning the things that must shortly come to pass, do not fail to have your name enrolled for these messages. By sending now and enclosing one dollar, you will be sent a copy of each message as it is printed. If you cannot spare a dollar, send what you can, have your name enrolled and send balance later. I am sure you will find these messages will prove a great blessing to you, I am,

Your Brother in Jesus,
S. R. HENDERSON.

P. S.—The following pastors have endorsed these messages as fundamentally sound and scriptural:

Rev. Benny Baggett,
LeBlanc, La.,

Rev. Norbert Benoit.
Branch, La.,

Rev. M. J. Baggett,
Dry Creek, La.,

Rev. H. E Gilbert,
Crowley, La.,

Rev. R. L. LeFleur,
Oakdale, La.,

Rev. F. C. Burks,
Evangeline, La.,

Rev. Arthur T. Morgan, Alexandria, La.

Send all orders to S. R. Henderson, Iota, Louisiana

Printed in the United States
55699LVS00001B/358-645